Super Smart Animals

Dolphins
Are Smart!

Leigh Rockwood

PowerKiDS press

New York

Published in 2010 by The Rosen Publishing Group, Inc.
29 East 21st Street, New York, NY 10010

First Edition

Editor: Amelie von Zumbusch
Book Design: Julio Gil
Layout Design: Ashley Burrell
Photo Researcher: Jessica Gerweck

Photo Credits: Cover, back cover (dolphin, horse, parrot, pig), pp. 9, 18 Shutterstock.com; back cover (chimpanzee) Manoj Shah/Getty Images; back cover (dog) Courtesy of Lindsy Whitten; p. 5 Heidi Grassley/Getty Images; p. 6 © Michael S. Nolan/age fotostock; p. 9 Shutterstock.com; pp. 10, 17 Jeff Rotman/Getty Images; p. 13 David Olsen/Getty Images; p. 14 VEER Renee DeMartin/Getty Images; p. 21 © James L. Amos/Peter Arnold, Inc.

Library of Congress Cataloging-in-Publication Data

Rockwood, Leigh.
  Dolphins are smart! / Leigh Rockwood. — 1st ed.
     p. cm. — (Super smart animals)
  Includes index.
  ISBN 978-1-4358-9398-6 (library binding) — ISBN 978-1-4358-9842-4 (pbk.) —
ISBN 978-1-4358-9843-1 (6-pack)
  1. Dolphins—Juvenile literature. 2. Dolphins—Psychology—Juvenile literature. I. Title.
  QL737.C432R636 2010
  599.53—dc22
                              2009035736

Manufactured in the United States of America

CPSIA Compliance Information: Batch #WW10PK: For Further Information contact Rosen Publishing, New York, New York at 1-800-237-9932

Contents

Dolphins Are Mammals

When you think about dolphins, you might picture them swimming playfully near boats or doing tricks at a water park. Dolphins spend their whole lives in the water. These playful animals look like big fish, so it may surprise you to learn that they are **mammals**. As all mammals do, dolphins breathe air. Dolphins must come to the water's **surface** to breathe. A dolphin breathes through an opening, called a blowhole, on top of its head.

Dolphins are considered smart animals. In **captivity**, dolphins have shown that they can learn tricks and **behaviors**. Scientists also discovered that dolphins have good problem-solving skills.

Because they are so smart, dolphins are easy to train. Dolphins can learn to do many tricks, such as jumping through hoops.

▶

Dolphin Species

Did you know that there are 36 species, or kinds, of dolphins in the world? Most dolphins live in the ocean. However, there are some species that live in freshwater.

Dolphins are related to whales. In fact, the world's largest dolphin, the orca, is sometimes called the killer whale. Another kind of dolphin, the spinner dolphin, is named for the way that it sometimes jumps and spins along the water's surface. One of the most common dolphin species is the bottlenose dolphin. This kind of dolphin lives in oceans around the world. It is the kind of dolphin you see most often at zoos and aquariums.

◄ This dolphin is a spinner dolphin. Spinner dolphins generally have white undersides. They live in warm oceans around the world.

Built for Swimming

Dolphins' bodies are built for swimming. They have flippers, fins, and strong tails with two **flukes**. Their smooth bodies help dolphins move through the water quickly. In fact, dolphins can swim as fast as 18 miles per hour (30 km/h). Since dolphins must come to the surface every few minutes to breathe, most do not dive very deep.

If dolphins need to come up for air, how can they breathe while they sleep? While sleeping, they float near the top of the water. Small **automatic** movements of their flukes push them to the surface so that they can breathe!

Dolphins push themselves through the water by moving their flukes up and down. They steer with their flippers.

The Dolphin's Life Cycle

Depending on their species, dolphins are fully grown between 5 and 13 years of age. A grown dolphin is 10 to 14 feet (3–4 m) long and weighs around 1,100 pounds (500 kg). A few years after they become adults, dolphins will **mate**. About a year after mating, the mother gives birth to one calf. The mother dolphin nurses her calf for most of the next two years.

Calves quickly learn to swim alongside their mothers. Calves also learn the sounds their mothers make. These sounds help calves find their mothers. The calves' own calls often sound a bit like their mothers' calls!

◄ Dolphin calves often swim very close to their mothers. This makes it easier for the calves to swim. It also keeps them from getting lost.

Pod Life

Dolphins live in groups called pods. Pods can have a handful of members or hundreds of members. A pod's size can change over time as groups of dolphins join or leave the pod. These smaller groups can be made up of mothers and calves, young adults, or adult males.

The pod swims, plays, and hunts together. Pod members work together to herd fish to make them easier to catch. Pods also work together to chase away **predators**. Pod members care for each other, too. If one member is hurt or sick, other members take turns helping that dolphin reach the water's surface to breathe.

Spinner dolphins, such as these animals, often live in large pods. Some spinner dolphin pods have more than 1,000 members!

▶

What's That Sound?

Dolphins **communicate** using sounds, such as clicks, whistles, and squeals. These sounds let nearby dolphins know where a dolphin is and how it is feeling. Each dolphin makes its own sound. This sound **identifies** it to other dolphins.

Dolphins also make sounds for **echolocation**. When using echolocation, dolphins make clicks. These send out sound waves. The waves move through the water and **bounce** back when they hit something. When a dolphin senses the returning waves, it can tell the size and location of the object the waves hit. Dolphins use echolocation to find food. They also sense predators using echolocation.

◀ **Scientists think that dolphins send out echolocation sounds through their melons, or foreheads. The animals likely sense returning sound waves in their lower jaws.**

Smart Hunters

Dolphins have clever ways of hunting **prey**. Dolphins often hunt by herding prey into a small space. They also force fish onto the beach so they can grab them without the fish getting away. Some bottlenose dolphins put sea sponges on the tips of their noses. This keeps their noses safe when they bump into rocks while they are hunting. Dolphins are also known to follow fishing boats. They hope to catch fishermen's unwanted fish!

Dolphins use their small sharp teeth to grab their prey. However, they usually swallow their prey whole. Most dolphins eat fish, octopus, squid, and shrimp.

This bottlenose dolphin has caught a reef octopus. Bottlenose dolphins often catch and eat between 15 and 30 pounds (7–14 kg) of food each day. ▶

Jumping and Spinning

   Some of the things dolphins are most known for are their playful spirits and their lively jumps out of the water. Bottlenose dolphins can jump more than 16 feet (5 m) out of the water before splashing down. Spinner dolphins jump and spin in circles before returning to the water.

   No one is sure why dolphins jump out of the water. Scientists have a few ideas. Some think dolphins may be looking for fish-eating birds. The birds could give dolphins clues about where to find food. Other people believe jumping may be a form of communication. A few scientists think that dolphins jump for fun.

◀ **These playful bottlenose dolphins are jumping out of the water backward! Dolphins can do somersaults and belly flops. They can also jump in pairs.**

Studying Dolphins

Some scientists study dolphins to learn about their lives. Scientists also try to apply what they learn about dolphins to other scientific areas. For example, the U.S. Navy studies dolphins' use of echolocation. They hope echolocation could help divers find things in the ocean. The Navy has also studied how dolphins' bodies stay warm in cold water to see if they can improve their diving gear.

Scientists study dolphins' social groups and communication, too. Learning about all parts of dolphin life can teach scientists more about how animals, including people, learn and communicate. It can also help us understand how communities work.

This scientist from Long Marine Laboratory, in Santa Cruz, California, is studying dolphins. She is trying to learn more about how they use echolocation. ▶

Dolphins and People

Dolphins need large spaces in which to swim, use their echolocation skills, and communicate with other dolphins. This makes dolphins unsuited to living in captivity, especially in water parks where they live in small pools.

The best place to see dolphins is in the wild, where they live with their pods and swim freely. Dolphins are curious and often swim near boats that come into their **habitat**. If you see a dolphin in its habitat, remember that it is one of nature's smartest animals. Feel lucky that you are getting a peek into the world of this super smart animal!

Glossary

automatic (aw-tuh-MA-tik) Done without being thought about.

behaviors (bee-HAY-vyurz) Ways to act.

bounce (BOWNS) To spring up, down, or to the side.

captivity (kap-TIH-vih-tee) A place where animals live, such as in a home, a zoo, or an aquarium, instead of living in the wild.

communicate (kuh-MYOO-nih-kayt) To share facts or feelings.

echolocation (eh-koh-loh-KAY-shun) A method of locating objects by producing a sound and judging the time it takes the echo to return and the direction from which it returns.

flukes (FLOOKS) Parts of a whale's or dolphin's tail.

habitat (HA-beh-tat) The kind of land where an animal or a plant naturally lives.

identifies (eye-DEN-tuh-fyz) Tells what something is.

mammals (MA-mulz) Warm-blooded animals that have backbones and hair, breathe air, and feed milk to their young.

mate (MAYT) To come together to make babies.

predators (PREH-duh-terz) Animals that kill other animals for food.

prey (PRAY) An animal that is hunted by another animal for food.

surface (SER-fes) The outside of anything.

Index

A
adults, 11–12
air, 4, 8

B
blowhole, 4
boats, 4, 16, 22

C
captivity, 4, 22
clicks, 15

E
echolocation, 15, 20

F
fish, 4, 12, 16
flukes, 8
freshwater, 7

H
habitat, 22

K
kind, 7

O
ocean, 7
orca, 7

P
predators, 12, 15
prey, 16

S
scientists, 4, 20
skills, 4, 22
species, 7, 11

T
tricks, 4

W
whale(s), 7

Web Sites

Due to the changing nature of Internet links, PowerKids Press has developed an online list of Web sites related to the subject of this book. This site is updated regularly. Please use this link to access the list: www.powerkidslinks.com/ssan/dolphin/